Capturing your memories to leave your legacy

7 steps to creating your book

Barbara J. Cormack

WRITERS EDGE
SERIES

Published by PenCraft Books Limited

Capturing your memories to leave your legacy

ISBN: 978-1-939556-23-3 (Kindle)
ISBN: 978-0692846995 (Print)
ISBN: 978-1-939556-24-0 (PDF)

First published: March, 2017 UK

Published by: PenCraft Books Limited
27 Old Gloucester Street, London WC1N 3AX, United Kingdom

Images used throughout this book are sourced from Pixabay, Dreamstime, 123RF, PresenterMedia, Shutterstock, or Alphaspirit | Dreamstime.com.

Contents

Capturing your memories to leave your legacy

Introduction

There is a lot of information available to you about your own history on the internet; but, writing about your own history gives you the opportunity to leave a legacy for your own family as well as a wider audience. It is a gift within you that you can share through your own creative writing.

Each person who creates a piece of text for someone else to read, listen to, or watch is an author. Whether you are writing a novel, a cookbook, a poem, a film or theatre script, an article, software program, multimedia, hypertext, help text, training material, or even a blog; you will be considered the author.

Business writing sometimes is seen in a different light as there maybe more than one person who has contributed to the writing; but in the same way each person who has contributed could be seen to be the co-author of the writing.

Educational writing? You are the author of all the papers that you write as part of your education.

An author is not a compiler, a translator, an editor, a copyist, or a copywriter. An author is simply someone who commits their thoughts to paper (actual or electronically) for others to read.

As an author you are writing; and writing is both an art and a craft that covers many genres. Each genre can bring entertainment, information, and knowledge to the person reading.

1

Capturing your memories to leave your legacy

There is a difference between the art of writing and the craft of writing. E.A. Bucchianeri said "Art is in the eye of the beholder, and everyone will have their own interpretation". This is important because the craft of writing (the actual doing) determines the art. In other words, the how you write will determine the interpretation by the reader.

Over the years there have been many well-known and respected writers. Each one providing their audience with one or more messages. To name a few of these; A.A. Milne, Beatrix Potter, Bob Proctor, Dale Carnegie, Dylan Thomas, Ernest Hemingway, J.K. Rowling, Jack Canfield, Nevil Shute, Shakespeare, Tony Robbins, William Smith, the biblical story tellers, and the list goes on. Whether the message is provided through fact or fiction, each of these writers has two things in common:
1.   Their motivation to share a story, their knowledge and/or information.
2.   Their writing system facilitating their writing process.

If writing is something that you have already made part of your life, this book may help you become more structured in your approach. However, if you are new to writing, this book will facilitate your book by showing you the 7 steps of book creation.

1 Understand the 'what', the 'why', and the 'who'

Each writer has a motivation to share his or her story, knowledge, or information.

TOPIC:

>What do you want to write about? You have a number of stories within you and it is important to understand what you want to write about in your book. i.e. topic, specific information, story following a particular genre. If you have more than one 'topic' make a list of all of them. Then select one topic for this book. You may select another and another, once your book is published.

REASON:

>What is your reason for sharing this knowledge or information or story? You can justify your reason by asking yourself 'why you want to write this particular book?'

SUCCESS:

>Your definition of your own success will determine your feelings when you see your final result. What is your own definition of success? Do you want to hold your own printed and/or electronic book in your hands? Do you want to make a change to other people's lives? Do you want to capture the imagination of others through creating a story? Do you want to use this book to share knowledge and information with clients, or students, or colleagues? Do you want to earn an income from your writing?

Capturing your memories to leave your legacy

AUDIENCE:

> It is important to understand your audience – who they are, where they are, and what they are looking for. There are so many opportunities today. It is important for you to know which other books and authors your audience enjoys, and where they find those books. This will also help you in marketing your book.
>
> A journal is confidential writing for your eyes only. A book is not! A book is to be read by other people – some of whom you know and some you do not know.
>
> For every book that is written a specific audience can be determined. For example, Jane Austen writes romance novels. She knew that there is was an audience who would read romance novels, especially those of her particular period of time.
>
> Who is your audience? Who are your readers?

You are unique, you want your writing to be original, and presented in your own unique style.

- What are the top 10 award-winning or bestselling books that are similar to the book that you want to write?
- Which current authors write the books that you love to read?
- Which current authors write the books that are similar to the book you want to write?
- Now that you have your list, check them out of Amazon, Nook, Kobo, etc. For each book scroll

down to the product details and find out the 'bestseller rank', which categories and sub-categories against which the book is registered (or in other words, which bookshelves will you find the book on; or which search engine words will you use), and genre.

Now that you know what you want to write about, your reason for wanting to write, and who your audience is; you can start to write a book that you will enjoy writing and will find you an audience who will enjoy reading it.

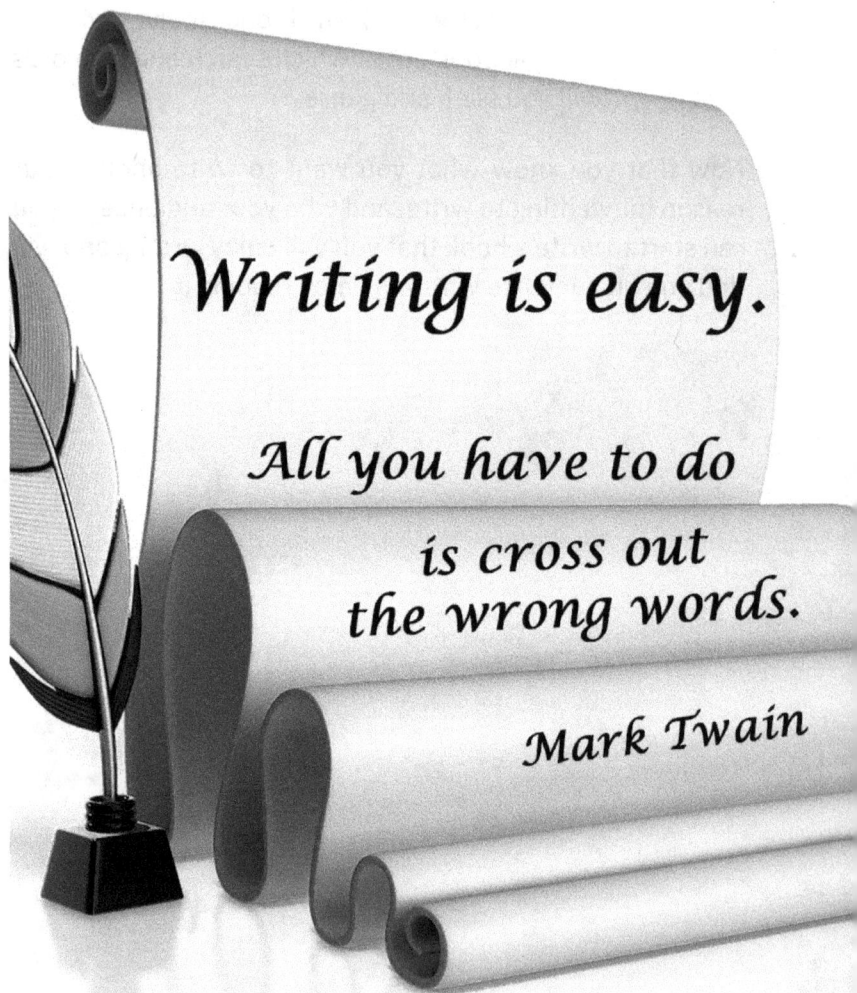

Writing is easy.

All you have to do is cross out the wrong words.

Mark Twain

2 Your writing system

Essentially the craft of writing is the arrangement of specific words and the use of grammar as tools to express your knowledge, information or story. It is a structure that starts with a beginning, has a middle, and concludes with an ending. Each word within each sentence builds your thoughts coherently in the form of a poem, prose, article, or a book.

Create your routine!

This is your KEY to your success! There are hundreds of suggested writing routines that can be found on the internet today. The secret to your success is to create the one routine that works for you.

ENVIRONMENT:

> You must be able to work in an environment that is quiet and has no distractions. Unplug the internet, switch off your phones (all of them), and tell people around you that you are not to be disturbed.

NOTES:

> Then use a journal to capture notes as you think about them. Your mind does not switch off and something you see or hear may trigger a thought in your mind about something you want to include in your book. Capture that thought NOW!

GOAL:

> Time or Number of Words – some authors will tell you they sit down to write a specific number of words a day; while others will tell you that they

allocate a specific number of hours per day. Whichever works for you is the right way forward for you. Which is it?

If you want to write for an hour a day – get your diary out and commit to when that hour will be each day.

If you want to write a specific number of words each day, how long will it take you to write those words? Get your diary out and commit to when that time will be each day.

PREPARATION:

What do you need to do before you go into your 'environment'?

If you need to take a cup of coffee, make it before you go into your environment.in. If you need to have a bathroom break, take it before you go into your environment. If you need to meditate, add this to your writing time and start with your meditation when you first go into your environment. Whatever it is that you need, do it before you start your writing.

RESEARCH TIME:

how do you want to do your research? Is this part of your allocated writing time or not? If it is, then you need to make sure that you have the time to both do your research as well as write for the time you have specified or the number of words you have committed to. If not, when will you do this research?

What research do you need to have completed before you can write the next section?

The key to your SUCCESS is creating your own writing routine!

Procrastination comes in many forms. Reading rather than writing is a great form of procrastination. Not having a clear routine is a form of procrastination. If you cannot make yourself accountable to yourself, find someone who can support you. For example, find someone who can be your coach, mentor, tutor/lecturer; it could be a colleague, or your partner/spouse. Whoever you select must be a motivator and be someone who is capable of motivating you.

Capturing your memories to leave your legacy

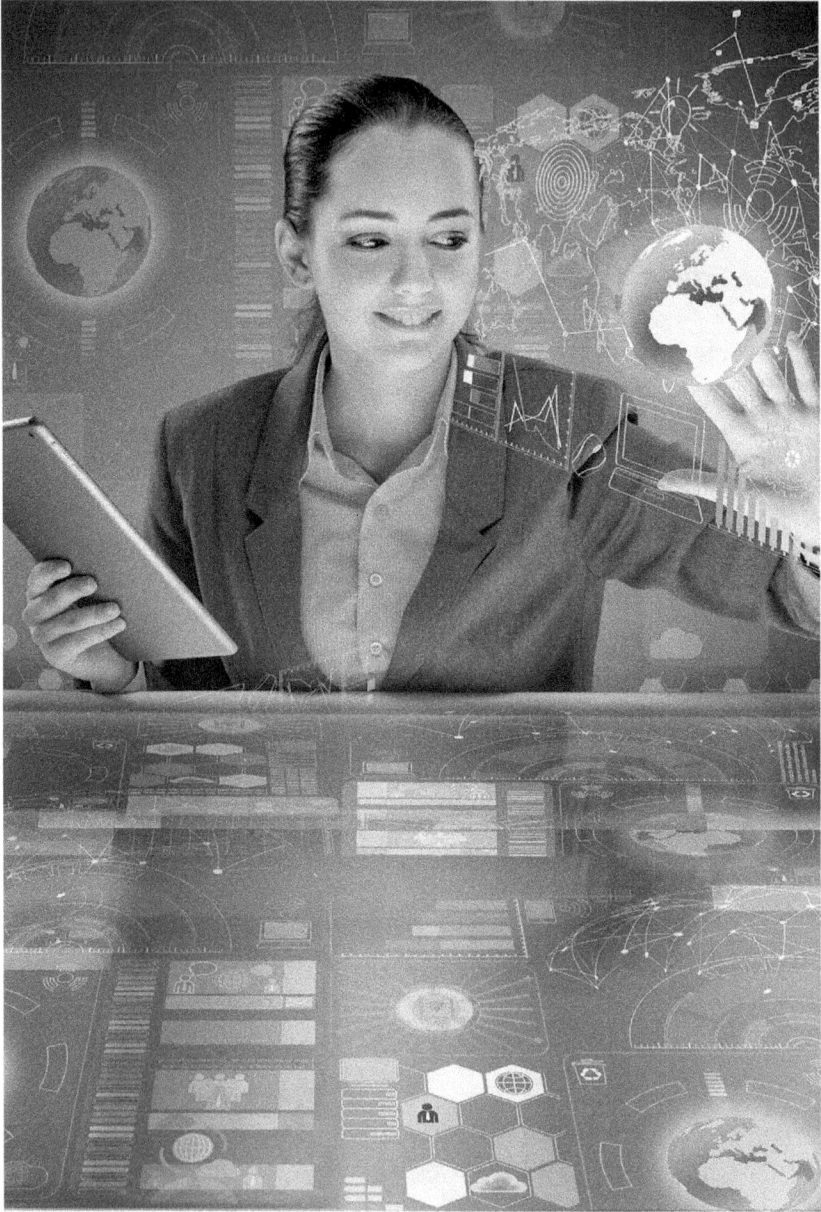

3 Research

In today's world of information sharing, there is always the question 'how much research did the author do before they published this information'?

Should you do any research? How much research should you do? Should you just write from the heart? The answer to these questions is that the research you do will depend upon the reason you are writing. If you are writing a novel that has no 'technical' information in it, then yes you can just write from the heart; although when you read about the months of detailed research Arthur Hailey did for each of his books, it does make you wonder – should you do some research?   Whereas if you are writing training material, then you will need to have done some previous learning, gained experience, and researched the topic. So the levels of research will be different.

Research can be seen as a distraction from actually writing; a delaying tactic; procrastination; or a reason not to start writing yet. It's plausible!

When you created your writing routine and you set your goal; in this goal only you will know how much research you want to do, and will do.

More information on research available in Successful Research, published as part of the Writers Edge series by PenCraft Books Limited.

Capturing your memories to leave your legacy

4 Conceptualise

Table of Contents

To really get your book to flow it is important to brainstorm your table of contents. Not only will this give you the opportunity to see how the topic flows from the beginning to the end, but also allow you to understand which specific elements of this topic you want to include.

When you start this process, write everything down. There is no right and no wrong way to do this. You can start by writing down what you believe your chapter headings will be, and then add the elements to each chapter, or you can brainstorm all the elements and combine them into chapters later. Some use a formal process called mindmapping to accomplish this same brainstorming process.

I find it's at this time when a mindmap is useful. A mindmap is simply a diagram which shows your elements collected together in chapters. It will show a relationship between each chapter, and can help you understand the flow of information.

Capture all your ideas, your thoughts, and information to include in your book. It does not matter how detailed your mindmap is or how long your list is. What is important is that you capture as much detail as possible.

Detail

Once you have your Table of Contents it is important to understand how much information you have for each

Capturing your memories to leave your legacy

element of each chapter.

Take each chapter and each element one at a time. Start to make notes about what information you have on each element and identify the information you may need to research.

It is important that you capture everything now; even if it's just a few words on the element to give you a guide later as to what you want to write about.

As you are working your way through the elements you may decide that an element is not required, or that one or more other elements could be combined. Sometimes you might find that you have a huge amount of information for one element and outline information for others. Whatever you decide, now is the time to pull together the outline for your book.

There are many different ways in which you can do this – using a mindmap for each chapter and adding more detail on each element, or using post-it notes on a white board, or making lists in Microsoft Word (or similar word processing software), or OneNote, or using software like Scrivener.

Research the open issues

Once you have captured all the information you have about your chapters and your elements, make a consolidated list of all the research you need to complete. Take the time out now to do that research and capture the important notes under each relevant element.

Only once you have collated all the information, table of contents, and notes, you ready to write your book.

Decision

Do you have the correct amount of information for each chapter?

You can spend hundreds or thousands of hours reading other books, research each element, and collating notes; but is it all needed?

Based on your understanding of your audience, what do they really want covered? Will you provide too much detail or have you got enough information to provide just the right level of detail in your writing?

Prepare to write

Step-by-step starting with the first chapter and first element, work your way through the book:

- Does the book flow from an introduction at the beginning to a conclusion at the end?
- Where you are using colloquialisms or technical terms or jargon, have you included a way in which you can explain in plain English (or the language of your book)?
- Have you got too much information about an element? What can you cut out?

Research shows that normally a book based on knowledge and information is around 175 pages. If you have too much information, consider how to introduce just the right level of detail, may be giving yourself the chance to create a sequel.

Set yourself targets. When you created your routine you were looking at your own time and your environment – now is the time to set writing targets. For example, when do you believe chapter 1 will be finished?

1. Chapter headings.
2. Each element in each chapter.
3. Outline notes to explain each element.

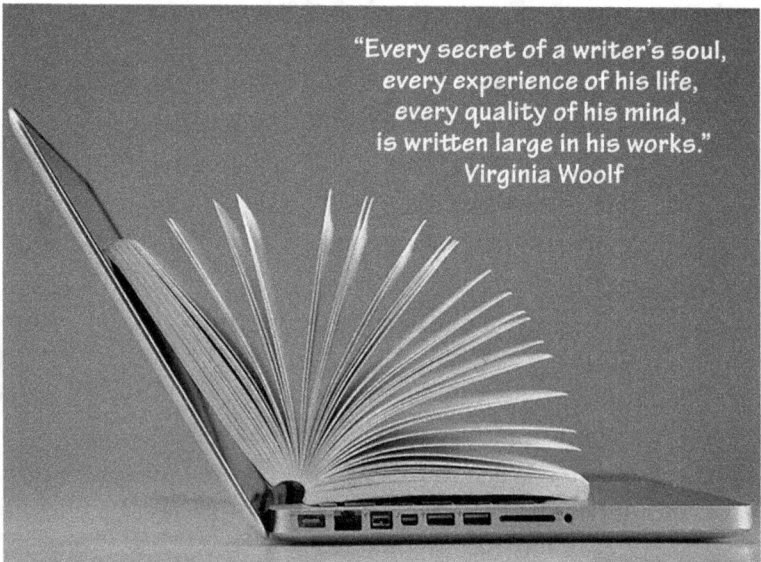

"Every secret of a writer's soul,
every experience of his life,
every quality of his mind,
is written large in his works."
Virginia Woolf

5 Write!

Be aware of the deadlines you set for yourself to write each chapter.

Remember that you are writing for your audience. You are not writing for yourself! It may help you to create a person in your mind who represents your audience, so that you can writer personally to that person.

Don't *assume* that the person reading your book has the same level of knowledge and information as you have. There is a balance in your explanations; you need to provide enough information without making it a rambling section that loses the attention of your reader.

Now turn your concept into your book.

In step 2 you created your routine – now is the time to make sure that your routine works for you.

Make yourself accountable. Celebrate small successes. Review the reasons for delays (which can be truly valid i.e. something important happening that you had no control over, or writing just truly takes you longer than you thought).

If you are finding that you are not meeting your deadlines, go back and think about your reasons for writing this book and your audience. What are the audience looking for and why are you writing this for them?

Now write! Put those first words on paper. You have done a lot of work already, so take chapter 1 and the first element, and start to expand on the notes you made.

You can do this either by physically writing your book or through dictating it. If you select to dictate it, either find someone who can transcribe your dictations; or select to use software that will create the written word.

The majority of writers I know or have researched have found that setting a writing schedule is the key to success. In step 2, I talked about setting yourself to write a specific number of words or to write for a specific period of time. Whichever works best for you is the one to select.

Don't worry about your language or your grammar. The first draft is your opportunity to capture your thoughts and notes in enough detail to publish the knowledge and/or information and/or story. During your review and editing step you can tidy up the language and grammar.

Monitor your progress. You know that you have a set number of chapters to write, and in each chapter you have a specific number of elements. You also begin to understand what progress you can make in each writing session. Therefore, you are able to monitor your progress. You can keep track of how far you are progressing against the concept you created in the previous step.

One word at a time is how your book will be achieved; and the only way to write one word at a time is to use your scheduled time to write. If you find that you are sitting at your computer and looking at a blank sheet of paper, pick up your notes and ask yourself 'if I was to verbally explain this to a colleague, what would I say now?' Write that down.

6 Review and Edit

"The only kind of writing is rewriting."
Ernest Hemingway.

Review

The reason I don't call this step re-writing is that I have a fear of reading what I have written or even listening to my own voice after I have recorded something. I find thinking about this step as a review of what has been written a more productive approach.

However, you want to think about this, it is important to now be your own critique. This review or critique is where the magic will happen. This is the chance you get to truly understand what you have said and what you meant. I know that when I've written a piece to record it, that I find myself looking at it before the recording and realising that what I've written will not make sense if I read it in the way I have written it.

My secret is to read out loud. I close my study door so that no-one else can hear what I'm saying and I read the material I have written. Have you put punctuations where it is needed? Have you provided adequate detail to explain your point? Does your writing flow successfully from the previous point and into the next point? Have you made assumptions which are not understood?

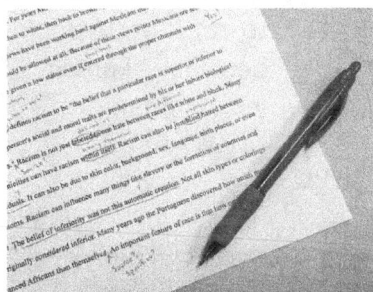

Capturing your memories to leave your legacy

Reasons for Reviewing

Reviewing your writing allows you:

GRAMMAR:
> correct your grammar.

CLARIFY MEANING:
> re-write sections that you may understand that someone reading it, may not.

FLOW:
> does the information flow correctly? Writing is fluid. It can be changed, shaped, and re-shaped until you, as the author, know it's the best you can make it. Richard Cormier said "The beautiful part of writing is that you don't have to get it right the first time, unlike, say, a brain surgeon."

DOUBLE EXPLANATION:
> have you explained the same item in two places differently?

AUDIENCE:
> does this book meet your audience's expectations?

> Be objective. Be critical. You want your audience to refer your book to others. You may want to become known for your knowledge and information.

TYPOS:
> fix the typing mistakes. It's distracting when you are reading a book that is full of typing mistakes, full of

20

spelling mistakes, and has no or very little punctuation.

Often you are in a hurry to publish your book, but it is important to remember that, your book can be a great success or not if the above items are verified. If you have rushed explanations, or put in half descriptions, or not validated the flow of information; then the first people reading your book may select to give you a low rating.

Re-writing

Re-writing takes time and it is that time that you put into your book that will make it the best seller that you can publish.

Harry Shaw said "Those unwilling to revise and rewrite are skipping a major step toward becoming better writers."

It is recognized that rarely in the first stages of writing can the author (experienced or first-time) produce a book that is well-constructed with language and grammar perfect. To achieve this takes time and patience.

Assistance

If, like me, you don't like reviewing your own work, you can always ask someone else to read it and provide you with their feedback.

If you have reviewed your book and either can't see what needs fixing; or can't see how to fix it; ask someone else.

It is also said that writing and reviewing are two completely different skills, which cannot be intermingled. Writing is the function of our creative brain, while reviewing needs to be the part of our analytical brain.

If you do select to ask for assistance and get someone else to read your first stage of writing, it is your decision whether you accept what they feed back to you or not.

Editing

Editing is not reviewing. Editing is sending your finished book to someone else, who will then read your book as though they were a member of your audience. They will provide you with detailed feedback which may include correction, condensation, expansion, organisation, questions, or other modifications. The editor's role is simply to make sure that your book is ready for your audience.

Selecting an editor is not always easy. Do you select someone you know or do you select someone you do not know? Do you select someone who understands your selected topic or genre, or do you select someone who has no understanding of your selected topic or genre?

What sort of editor do you need? Someone who is involved in your book from the beginning or someone who will only read it once it is ready for publication?

What sort of interaction do you need? An editor who can help you through every step of the way, or someone who will read your book as a member of your audience?

What sort of experience should your editor have? This is a more difficult question and the answer really should be driven from who your audience is. For example, if your audience is only people who know the topic of the book; then having an editor who understands the topic may bring more benefit. Whereas if your audience is anyone – people who have no knowledge of the topic to people who have an in-depth knowledge of your topic, then selecting an editor who has no knowledge of your topic may be the right editor for you.

Whoever you select, it is important that you give them clear guidance as to what you are looking for. Having said that, their role is clearly there to help you create the best book you can write.

Capturing your memories to leave your legacy

7 steps to publishing your book

Research

Conceptualise

Writing System

What, Why, Who

Publish!

Review & Edit

Write!

WRITERS EDGE

Barbara J. Cormack

7 Publishing

The final step allows you to take your writing and make the last decisions you need to make to enable you to publish:

- Book Title
- Book Sub-title
- Cover
- Book Description
- Book Genre, Categories, Sub-categories
- Author Description

If you have included images in your book, have you got the right permission to use them?

Your book title is often the first thing that your prospective audience see. This is followed closely by your book cover. It is important that you select the right title and that your cover is striking. When you consider that in 2015; 653 million books were published of which 204 million were eBooks; how does your prospective audience select your book? In your specific genre where you are not known to the person looking for a book, it is your title (and sub-title) and cover that will attract that person.

Your book description (often only 350 words or less) will give your audience an understanding of what you have written about. It is important that this description is specific and provides enough detail to make that person click the 'buy me' button. There is a lot of information on the internet about how to write the description, but I always suggest that you look at what others in your field/genre have written.

Capturing your memories to leave your legacy

Your own author description is as important as the book description. Put interesting information into your author description that provides a reason to buy the book.

In conclusion, you are capturing your memories for a reason, correct? As you send your book to be published, celebrate that you are leaving your legacy that few others have accomplished!

About PenCraft Books Limited

PenCraft Books, *your* ally in fulfilling *your* dream.

Stress Relief:
We created PenCraft Books because the learning curve that we had to overcome, as authors ourselves, was so steep and so totally unrelated to finishing the book and successfully selling the book in the marketplace. The stress of figuring out how to get the book finished was intense enough without having to learn new skills to get the book into the various formats for online reading and hardcopy versions, to select the correct distribution channels, to organize the marketing of the finished book.

Authors Asked For:
We talked with many authors and discovered a common theme...Authors need some support...otherwise all authors are really working by themselves...isolated and alone. The authors indicated that they need three types of support:

1. Personal Mentor: they *wished they'd had a personal mentor when they first started writing.* Someone who cared and had the expertise to guide them along the path from original idea; to beating the dreaded procrastination, overcoming limiting self-beliefs right through to seeing their work in print. Essentially, we help them become authors and achieve a finished manuscript.

2. Marketing: It's said that *writing a book is the easy part; it's the marketing of it when the real work starts.* That's why PenCraft helps its authors stand out in a crowded market place with a marketing strategy to reach the widest possible audience and

achieve maximum sales.

3. Publishing: they wished they could simply turn this process over to someone who could get the book published without the inherent stress. PenCraft prepares the finished manuscripts so they're available for readers both physically in bookstores, and on-line.

PenCraft, *your* coach in publishing *your* book...to help you reach *your* dream of writing your book

www.PenCraftBooks.com

www.ingramcontent.com/pod-product-compliance
Lightning Source LLC
Chambersburg PA
CBHW060706280326
41933CB00012B/2326